Harry Borno

DADOU MY UNIVERSE

Poetry

Author and translator's notes

"Dadou My Universe" is the English version of my first poetry book: "Dadou Mon Univers", a collection of love poems, written in French, illustrated with family pictures and a selection of my oil on canvas paintings, which was published through Ingramspark in September 2018.

In this new edition, I strived and was able to tailor the word to word translation of the French, to create an artwork that preserves the meaning and captures the tone and the essence of the original. One poem: "Prayer" redesigned completely the French: "Mauvais temps", (meaning "Bad weather") that I could not render in English to my satisfaction, and I added "Solar eclipse" and two paintings: "Haitian merchants" and "Deserted beach".

Dadou My Universe

All rights reserved
Copyright © 2019 by Harry Borno

ISBN: 978-0-578-56907-9

No part of this publication may be reproduced, stored in a retrieval system, or transmitted in any form or by any means electronic, mechanical, photocopying, recording, or otherwise, without the written permission of the author or publisher.

Table of Contents

Preface	1
Introduction	7
My universe	15
Brown rose	16
Romance	17
New Moon	19
When the storm is over	20
Dreamland	24
Delight	26
For you	28
Reverie	30
Nocturne	32
Letter to Dadou	33
Possession crisis	34
The sea	35
Sunset	36
My love	38
She	41
Solitude	45
Hope	46
Happy Mother's Day	47
For Helen	48
The marriage	53
Elegy	57
Premature hibernation	61
Prayer	63
January 12, 2010	65
Omnipotent	68
Solar eclipse	70
My sun	72
Epitaph	74

Preface

"A man like so many others, yet so different from others!" When my phone rang, I had the reflex to pick it up feverishly, especially since this call from Tarpon Springs, the space where Dr. Harry Borno lives, whom I admire and love with all my heart, announced me that finally he had made the ultimate decision to publish his collection of poems dedicated to his wife, Dorothy, my cousin, whom he venerates with all his soul. I could not help shouting: "Let me preface your masterpiece." I waited so long for this moment.

You have certainly read "TRISTAN and ISEULT, ROMEO and JULIETTE". But this collection of poems, created in filigree of all seasons of a unique life, dedicated to a peculiar woman, has nothing to envy to these novels with rose water. It will move you, if only by the sincerity, the simplicity and the expression of the artist's confession of love colored with notes of appreciation, admiration, respect, total trust, rare in some husbands in love.

Two passions dominate this nature of a deeply human, sensitive, intelligent man: his love for his wife and children and his unparalleled dedication to his patients, who trust him undeniably. Artist in his spare time, his painter's fingers fix on his canvas the portrait of his beloved wife, Dorothy, and reveal his ability to portray a marvelous sunset, a flowery nature.

The delicate touch of his inspiration pays homage to the superb Caribbean beaches highlighting the beautiful sites of Haiti, its country of origin.

Dr. Harry Borno's poem collection exudes a tender and passionate song, all the unconditional love he feels for his wife Dorothy and their children.

I pay tribute to a man, a husband, a father, a professional, who through his life has served as a model for generations of all ages and who is an ICON.

Marie R. R. Monique Souvenir

*Dadou
My Universe*

My Universe

Dorothy Dasque Borno
My Universe

Hibiscus

Introduction

This booklet is dedicated to you, to thank you for sharing my life, giving it a meaning and having adorned it with these wonderful children I love very much. Better than verses, it is an outbreak and flowering of this seed of love those who have participated in my existence and my education, and you have sown in my heart.

I would like this bouquet, freshly gathered in the parterre of our conjugal and social life, to remain forever blossomed and continue to embalm every minute of your days, while revealing the deepest of me: what I lived and felt and did not express,

what I say aloud, every day, but whose resonance is too weak to break the silence,

what I try to communicate often by gestures but remains frozen in indifference.

This sheaf of love, I join you to offer it with all my heart to your godmother, Gogotte Balmir, born Augusta Denis, and to all who, in one way or another,

> *contributed to our happiness;*
> *to my cousin,*
> *my friend,*
> *my brother,*
> *my father,*
> *Dr. Serge Balmir, who opened me the future*
> *and thought me the alphabet of life,*
> *to whom I owe, for the most part,*
> *what I am today;*

*to our children: Harrison, Natasha and Allain,
for their love and support;
to my dear brother, Gaston Borno;
to my mother, my father, my aunts, my uncles, my godmother, in loving memory;
to my cousin, my sister, Rosemarie Balmir;*

in summary, to all those, who will sacrifice a moment of their tumultuous life to look at these flowers and smell their perfume.

*If, at the end of the day, this collection of art - which is far from perfect and has no claim to rise to the height of the works of the masters of Haitian and foreign poetry - was able to inspire those who lament a broken union, and help them, somehow, to unite the fragments;
if these poems could serve as the last gust of wind that revives love in whatever form,
wherever it blooms,
where it does not grow and especially
when it fades,
when it is dying,
my wishes would be fulfilled.
To finish, a big thank you to everyone who encouraged and supported me.*

Harry Borno.

*Dadou
My Universe*

"You are a pure marble in the circle of my heart"
Michel-Ange Hyppolite

∞∞

"I prefer you to everything worth living and dying ..."
L. Aragon.

∞∞

O you
Light
Reason
Life engine
Love
My everything

For your wisdom
your kindness
your goodness
the mutilated moments
and the sacrifice of time

For our mirrors
the follies
the challenges
eternity.

∞∞

Dadou
My Universe

My universe

You came this morning
and everything changed suddenly.
Now all I pass near
bears your lips and models your figure.
You are this new North,
this fifth pole, where are measured
all GPS and compass
You came and reinvented all
You gave me another sky, drew new horizons
and my heart knows no rhythm
but your romance and your whim
Any word, any thrill, any sound,
echoes your voice.
Sometimes I see the end of the world
when you get angry or sulk.
Your silence is gall,
a block of lead on my chest
heavier than all the world sufferings.
I'm nothing without your smile, so warm
that it kindles flames and revives ashes,
nothing without your new moon eyes
when at night I gaze at you.
I am nothing without you,
this human marvel,
that makes one dream.
I am nothing, nothing
without you, my universe.

Brown rose

I still see you
little star fallen from the clouds
this beautiful summer day
your face like a rose petal on your white bodice
You had rekindled hope
and brought the world back to life
Little brown angel in green linen trousers
you came from a lost paradise
Your look had weighed on my heart
like a bird on a dead stem
You were very pretty more beautiful
than the goddess of blue dreams
and sleepless nights

I still see you
little flower with red satin lips
cheeks still beaded with morning dew
You hatched that night where
birds were singing Julio Iglesias
Your petals had perfumed the Pittsburgh Gardens
and colored its mountains and rivers
I still see you

Today you are still very pretty
more beautiful than the goddess of blue dreams
and sleepless nights
I love you well
little bouquet of brown roses

Romance

Come
stop playing this Latin melody
Rather let me hear
your cries
your sobs
your whisperings
your outflows
Sing me the song of your trances
Tonight I want to hear you

Come
empty everywhere
in your heart
in my heart
turn off the lamps
turn off the moon
let only your smile
and your eyes shine
Tonight I only want you

Come
Tonight I want to hear you
Let's play again and again
the scenes of our life
our unleashed love
Tell me those broken words
you whispered that night
when I became you

Walk me through the forest of your hair
Make me smell your breath
your perfume
Tonight I only want you

Please
Tonight repaint your way
this monstrous landscape
these chimerical faces
Stall the earth
Stop the time
Stop everything
even this Latin song I love so much
Let me instead listen
to your stepping
your sighs
your heartbeat
Tonight I want to hear you.

∞∞

New Moon

(Premenstrual syndrome)

I will not ask you why your lovely look
became dim so early
and night came down this morning

I will not try to rekindle your smile
and chase off your face
those shadows that have darkened my heart
Nor will I try to kiss you
and clear your frown
that has aged me suddenly

And above all
I will not repeat
that I love you
that I adore you
that life is you

I will keep quiet
for fear of unleashing this thunder
that scolds in you and is ready to destroy
I'll go slowly to my corner
without your lips
without your hug
without your warmth
hoping that the storm has passed

When the storm is over

Tomorrow when the storm
that pounded our heart is over
and we're again entwined
Tomorrow when your smile that is reborn
will have chased away the shadows and the clouds
I'll tell you a big secret
I will tell you that I love you
much more than myself
and that life is you
you who sing and dance
you who walk and bounce
like a stream
in the contour of the rocks.

Life is you who look at me
and speak to me,
it's when you wake me up
with a kiss of red flower on the lips.
Life is you who take me in your arms
and tell me that you love me.

Tomorrow I will tell you that I die
every time you cry
and that death
is anything that breaks your heart
the torments
the worries
the unfulfilled dreams and desires
Death is the last word you say
before sinking into your bed
it's when you turn your back on me
without a kiss
It's this monster
that I create
and that inflames your eyelids
It's the cold of your absence
and the weight of your silence
like a neck lock
a bulwark
Death is the twilight of your eyes
and the simple fear of awakening
without the rays of your presence

Tomorrow I will tell you
I only know you
and that emptiness begins
where your tracks get lost
It is the satisfaction of a desire
and the release of emotion
without your cries
It is a Chopin's Nocturne
without the sound of your voice
It's the summer starry sky
without the brightness of your eyes
It's the breeze of serene nights
without your breath
without your aroma
It is the rose just hatched
without the dampness of your lips
and the pearls of your forehead

Nothingness is sleeping
without your body
without your fever
Like death
it is life without your love
without you.

Tomorrow when the storm is over
and we are entwined
I will hold your face
in the palm of my hands
and I will tell you
that I love you
that I love you very much
much more than myself.

∞∞

Dreamland

When the children are grown up
I will take you to this country
where the stars are warmer
than your caresses
In this country
where jasmine blooms on mango trees
and the swallows dance the "Compas"

I will take you to this country
where people are sweet
as sweet as your child's smile
I will bring you far from this world
far from this golden hell
in this land of eternal spring
where you'll wake up to the sound of cocoricos
under the burning kisses of the sun

When you arrive in this country
you will sleep in the open air
in the shade of almond trees
with the locust violins
and the look of the moon

I will take you to this country
when the children are grown up

Top: Taxi, "Moulin sur mer". Bottom: Market, Haiti

Delight

Alone with you
I am looking at you lying in bed
like a flower in an overturned pot.
Your cheeks of pink petals
and your eyelids filled with dreams
have taken me away to unknown sites.
I'm thinking of the random that bound us
and the happiness you gave me
Thinking of the sweetness of life
life with you and the children
life with all
I'm thinking of you
Thinking about everything.

Alone with you
I'm staring at you
in the hollow of the silence
broken only by your heartbeat
and your breathing
Imagining with anxiety
the world without you
the tear of your loss
and the immensity of your emptiness.

Alone with you
I am admiring you
and wishing to abort the day you would go
like a bird
with the faded memories
I am trying to escape the time
you would throw away my shriveled heart
like a long-crumpled paper
in your palm.

Alone with you
I am contemplating you lying in bed
Thankful for life
life with you and these parts of us
life with all
Grateful and happy to exist
with you
in you
And I glorify the moment.

∞∞

For you

For you
I would invent another state
where your desires will be laws
and your reveries will have no bounds
a world without storm
without the winter freeze
a world where trees will produce love
and the avalanche will drain sufferings.

For you
I would undo the confusion of Babel
for humans to understand
the language of peace and harmony.
I would build another land
full of your dreams and light
where your smile will shine
and misery will be vanished.

For you
I would form a big bouquet of your past
and beautiful memories
to offer to those who are suffering
those who despair
and I would erase from your mind
the scars of your youth
and everything that breaks your heart

For you
I would remix
the melodies and the rhythms
you much enjoy
into a song full of sweetness
where your voice
your cries
your sighs
will make forte and crescendo
a piece of love
for every heart to rejoice

For you
I would destroy all the monsters
and the nightmares of our life
to create another world
the world of your dreams
and your fantasies.

∞∞

Reverie

No
I am not thinking about affairs
I'm thinking of you
I'm thinking of us
thinking of our love
its flower
and sweet fragrance
I'm looking for a formula
the formula of water or sap
that strengthens and eternizes

I'm thinking of the couples
who are trying to patch up violated vows
and holed dreams
those beloved and the unfortunates
who are carrying a broken heart
in a chest ready to burst

I'm thinking of all those
seeking the fragments of a love
buried in the mist of time
I'm thinking of you
and the nights spent
in the winter of my absence

No
it's about you
your velvet touch and lips
your dancing legs and hips
It's about you
and all the joy
you adorn my life with
your caresses
your kisses
your delights
I'm thinking of you
I'm thinking of us

∞∞

Nocturne

I like these moments
where time stops
and the world dies
when I do not see too far
no further than the screen of your eyes
where our passions play out.

I like these moments
when our shadows merge
and we forsake all identity.

I like when I lose my mind
and can only speak
and understand your language.

I like when you are smiling
I like when you're enjoying
I like when you love me.

Letter to Dadou

Forgive me for ruining this love concerto,
for having played this discordant note.
Forgive me for wasting time,
life already short.

You know I love you,
I love you dearly, much more than myself.

I love you like you are
and would never dream
of hurting you,
hurting me!
For remember I am not myself.
I exist only through you
and live between you.
I only feel what you feel
and I die every time you suffer.

Love
Forgive me for ruining the concert.
Come back
Forget

Life is inert
where you are not

Possession crisis

On your azure shore
wrecks which gnaw at my heart.
Your wave memories invade me
dig me and uncover treasures
that blind our moon.
Ha!
How to delete this slice of the past
without destroying you and erasing me,
you who made it a fragment of yourself
and me who exist and live but in you?

We keep renewing the promises of love,
but still, I'm worried,
jealous of stars of your dreams
where I do not act
and I am miserable
when I leave your fantasies.

It's foolish!
It's crazy!

But what can I do?
Prisoner of your love and your charm
I depend on you like your shadow,

I die every time you walk away.

The sea

For having received me
like the sea welcomes the torrent
with all its turbulence
and cold stream
the fragmented song of mountain adventures
and the broken rhythm of the rocky trails

For having sacrificed your candor and your serenity
shared your warmth
your immensity
your treasures
and your joys

For having donated the most precious of you
and having perpetuated me
through these children
who look like us
and whom I love

For having loved me
cherished me
and making me reign
over your kingdom
I thank you
and owe you my life

Sunset

You caressed me with your full moon eyes
and suddenly drew me to your horizons
my heart quite deserted
except for this intimate site occupied by your world.

Right there
everything is yours
and reminds you:
the beach sand where you left your bare feet
and the map of your feminine gait,
your summer breeze hands on my back
the tides that model your figure.

Everything reminds you on my shore
where the flora is an outbreak
of our love in flood
a bloom of your spring
a shower of roses
with every movement of your lips

Everything
Everything is yours on my beach
where the waves
draw your white dress
and the folds of your skirt.

This time at least
I'd like to abort your winter
and perpetuate the sublime moment
when your crescent smile mows the night.

I love you,
the only star in my darkened sky.
I invite you once and for all to stay
Stay with me
I love you as you are.

We will renew the promises of love
in the flight of the cloud
that caresses your face
and your sunset cheeks.

My love

Because you reinvented the world
and taught me to see all
through the prism of your immensity
Because you are at the end of everything
and gave me
what dream and fantasy cannot create

Because all my life rests on your heart
I'm bringing you my love
as pure as a child soul
at his first communion
my limitless love
crazy like our first kisses
as big as your clear sky look
more tenacious than those shores
where the waves are shattered

Because you love me
I'm bringing you my perennial love
as warm as the summer of your tenderness
my love of red flower
with the sap as intense
as the blood of your heart
my love that will not fade

Because it's you
I'm giving you my love forever.

To
Hélène and Antoine
(Loving memory)

Dorothy Dasque at 3 years old

She

She, Dadou,
with her sweet smile
and cheeks of brown roses,
was born in the moonlight,
an evening of fiesta at your flowering heart
on this unique summery night,
when your passions were doing wonders.

She, "Dadie", your kind flower,
has the scent and color
of the most beautiful pieces
of your dreams
and in the veins
all the sap of your full-blown love.
She has the softness of the breeze
that caresses and relaxes
the sweetness of the sun
that colors my morning
She is at the end of the dark days,
the sunshine when it rains in my life.

I thank you, dear parents,
for her wisdom of time.
Many thanks, mother and father
for having raised her proud,
head high as the statue of liberty,
and adorned her
with all the cream of your beauty.

Thanks, thanks,
father and mother
for having conceived her
with all your love at its best!

*Left to right: Antoine, Hélène Dasque,
Dorothy & Harrison Borno*

Dadou
My Universe

From left to right: Harrison, Natasha, Allain Borno

To our children gone for college

Solitude

Since you left the childhood home
the rain is ticking our flanks wide open
We are barely floating on waves of sadness
which have flooded our life.
Our heart is bogged down
up to the youngest to clear the valves.

Like roses amputated buds
we're suffering and waiting anxious
for the breakthrough of the stars
Who cares if the sunset occurs
at the south side of the horizon?
At any cost you must hatch your dreams

The future is blinding
and the freedom inebriating
A river of tears has hollowed our cheeks.
Who cares?
Nothing matters.
Nothing but what it takes
to reach the goal

The night today is very thick
but dawn is already
at the corner of the eyes.

To the broken couples and lovers

Hope

Don't worry about the lightning
that's tearing your darkened sky.
It has the fire that will mend your heart
and ignite your smile.
Faded promises will renew
and shine with as much glow
as the wishes of your first dates.
The aborted dreams will be reborn
and fulfilled the same way you enjoyed the past
Like the star that aurora hunts
yet faithfully returns to the gala of the night
the time of caresses will return
Will finally shine the moment when
You'll offer each other a bouquet of forgiveness
in a vase of oblivion
And all this storm will be nothing
but a bad nightmare.
Your love will not fade.
An intense season as vibrant as the spring of your life
will revive its petals and spread its scent
beyond the mountains of misfortune.

Do not worry about the weather
that's ravaging you and tearing your heart apart
Your love is alive
deeper than the abyss that carries you away.
Your love will not fade.

Happy Mother's Day

To you, dear mother
for your love without borders
and your infinite goodness

To you lantern of our life
source of eternal light
and constant kindness

For our step
you guided
our need
you help fill
everything
that bears
your fingerprints

From the deepest
part of our heart
find our promises
of love and faith

To you, dear mother
to celebrate your day
and thank you for your wonders
our bouquet of red flowers

For Helen

You're gone mother
but you're not dead
You will never die
The memory of your presence
as sweet as a summer breeze
will stroll us a long time yet
It will star our dark nights
in the cold of your absence

Everywhere will shine your smile
your contagious smile
your calm wave-smile
your smile that awakens
like a ray of sunshine
your warm smile
ardent as our love for you
Your smile will ignite your dust
and make you circulate
in the galaxy of our life
just like the stars of the universe

You will not die
you who have rocked us so often
you who have poured on us
all your tenderness
The seed of your kindness will blossom
and its flowers that are embalming
our entire space will defy infinity and time

Tonight, it's raining in our mired heart
But tomorrow when the storm has passed
and our tears will have drained the mess
we will wake up from this big nightmare
for you're not dead
you will never die
Your kindness is eternal.

Right to left: Hélène D. Dasque & her sister Augusta Denis Balmir

Dadou
My Universe

Harry and Dorothy Borno

The marriage

We came together
Like two separate roads merged at the crossing
living their paths, their friends, their landscapes
and joining for a common destination.
Each of us sacrificing the memories,
our youth, interests and personal attractions,
we gave up our course for a convergence
to a horizon of promise and happiness.

Every grain of my sand had taken your color
and penetrated the cement of your immensity.
I brought you the brightness
of my sky and its serenity
You gave me your tenderness
and its decanted flow,
your streets washed,
deserted of past follies
and anything that encumbers our union.
Our love had the fragrance of reinvented life
your deep love
my ardent love as warm
as the light of your eyes
that had brightened the infinite
and colored the future

Together we had crossed many deserts
and enjoyed mountains of pleasures
Together we had explored the cities of love
and built our three beautiful monuments.
Always allied we had overcome misfortunes
and savored the delights of nature.

Today we continue the journey hand in hand
launching into the future
like an interplanetary rocket
approaching steadily the realm of our dreams,
despite the bad weather
despite the whims of nature
despite the wear of time and habit.
We keep resisting to incoherent forces
determined to stay welded
our heart beating in a honeymoon
constantly renewed.

And still I do not regret coming to you
and having united for this adventure
towards a horizon of promise and happiness.

Thanks for having welcome me
with all my traffic jams,
my imperfections and my accidents.
Thanks for having made me reborn.

I owe you for repainting life in your own way.
For exposing to me its whole anatomy.
I now know how to dissect its elements.

Life is your smile that stars my nights
and brightens the mornings.
It's your figure, your gesture
that outline my landscapes and my shores.
It's your voice where resonates
all the music I like.
It's your love: the sum of all my passions.
    Life is you, my universe.

∞∞

Dr. Frantzie Balmir Beauvais
May 12, 1963 - August 26, 2012

Elegy

For Frantzie

You did not have to leave so soon
Petite Caribbean flower
with tamarind eyes and cinnamon petals
You who had barely hatched
and your mother and father baptized
wonder of their love.
You should not have closed so soon
Petite Caribbean flower
You who were embalming our lives
You who were coloring the days
of your debilitated parents
You who were their real right hand.

You should have stayed open
a little bit longer for your sisters
your husband
your boy
your relatives and friends
you were animating
with the beats of your melodious
and warm heart

You should have stayed a little bit longer
to contemplate hatching and flowering
those love seeds you planted
in the heart of your patients
and those around you.

Petite Caribbean flower
with tamarind eyes and cinnamon petals
You did not have to leave so soon
and let down your sweet dreams
You who loved nature and life so much
You who fought death with all your strength
You who were planning
to revolutionize MEDICINE
You should have stayed a little bit longer

When we say goodbye last week
I did not know that this hug
in which you put all your affection for me
was the last one.
Today, I try to comfort myself with the thought
that you left us to embalm another place
that may need your wisdom, your talent,
your love, much more.
I resign myself to the idea that you are not faded.

Petite Caribbean flower
with tamarind eyes and cinnamon petals
you will continue to beautify and refresh
our life forever.
You will never fade.
For your brilliance
your tenderness,
your goodness
are eternal.

August 29, 2012

To
Our daughter
Diagnosed with Leukemia

Natasha Elizabeth Borno
April 2, 1985 – July 7, 2015

Premature hibernation

Beautiful, brilliant, solitary flower of our garden
Our entire life shattered
when winter arrived
on this wonderful summer day
and forced your hibernation.
Neither you who were enjoying
the fruity and floral festival
nor we who were contemplating the harvest
were ready for this life adventure.

Watching you slip into this cavern of darkness
without a path to moonlight
has been very painful and terrifying.
Just as devastating has been
the show of your wilting
and shedding of your petals
favorite Indian attire you had just worn
for this festival of light and color.
We are now living the anxiety
of seeing days without sunshine
learning the agony of a season in transition
fighting sudden change
under the stress
and suffering of waiting for rebirth.

Our whole life turned upside down
when winter arrived this summertime
and forced your hibernation

We were not ready for your pilgrimage
but we accepted it as a test of faith
as the ransom for your anticipated rebirth,
as a reminder that
if the Almighty is always merciful
and never allows sorrow without comfort
nothing good happens
no creation takes place
there is no redemption, no salvation
without personal effort
without determination to succeed
without self-sacrifice and penance
That's why,
as macabre and depressing going dormant is
at a time when nature is celebrating
at a time when life is in full swing
at a time when there are so many dreams to fill
so many stars to pick
at a time when we only think of enjoying,
we will remain hopeful, comforted
to know this will be the last hibernation.
For the Spring is not far with its miracles of life
It will bring about renewal
The world will be reborn
You will wake up and emerge fresh
stronger, brighter and prettier
hardier than ever
very well acclimatized

Oct. 2012

Prayer

Lord, don't know why
got cloudy our sky,
why suddenly
this rainy day.

Don't know, Lord,
why our life has stalled,
why all's turning sour,
why this blizzard in full summer.

Please tell us
Lord Jesus
if there is a curse
in the house.

For we don't know
why so much sorrow,
don't understand
why our world has fallen.

Please tell us, Lord, why,
why the tide got so high.
Our boat is sinking.
Please, Lord, give us your blessing.

Sailboat of Haiti

January 12, 2010

I am a survivor of the January 12, 2010 earthquake
much luckier than thousands of compatriots,
relatives, friends who saw their homes crumbled
their landscapes reduced to memories
and their dreams dissipated in the mist of dust.

Like those who remain the witnesses
and tangible evidences of the disaster,
like those who live overseas
in the nostalgia of a past torn
and a future aborted
I am a survivor, say a living dead,
an injured bird, flying broken wings,
the heart cracked by the earthquake jolts
that reached him across the lands and waters
up to his refuge abroad.
Yes, I am a survivor, lucky
much more than those who remain trapped
in the enclave of hopeless dreams
haunted by the drama of a recurrence
Those who are crying missing family members, friends
Those sleeping with an empty stomach
Those who do not have a roof
Those who are swimming in the mess
Those who now live in tents at the mercy
of bad weather, rape and the carelessness
of the ones who have ignored the lessons.

My entire roots disturbed, limbs weakened
Pieces of the past scrambled
Compass lost
I live today in the space of a memory
a foggy one attached to the ends of dreams
collapsed dreams
aborted dreams
disabled dreams
militant dreams
surviving dreams, dreams, dreams...

Surely, I am a very lucky survivor
luckier than my compatriots who lost everything:
their harvest and long-life trophies
their roots and old-time links
even the energy of hope
Hope for rebirth
hope for a better tomorrow
hope for a Haiti renewed, reinvented
more beautiful and prosperous
A Haiti where order reigns
where everyone has the right of quotation
where every Haitian counts
where life is respected and appreciated
where love blooms
and avalanche drains unconsciousness
A Haiti where health and peace reign
A Haiti where we will love to live.
It's true, I'm a lucky survivor
Luckier than those who lost everything.

As grateful and comforted as those
who survived the earthquake
and at least have saved
the lantern of hope.

Haitian merchants, 16 x 20, oil on canvas.

Omnipotent

I am all yours
Turn me into what you want
a monster or an angel
Tear me apart with a stormy mood
or cover me with the petals
of your full-blown love.

Turn me into anything at your will.
Make me happy like your pillow
or as miserable
as this mirror in your drawer.
Fire my passions
or turn off my desires
whenever you want.
Kill me with indifference tonight
bring me back with a smile
when you wake up
Your tenderness is always magic.

You can make of me all you want.
After all, I did not exist
before I met you.
I owe you everything:
my life purpose,
my happiness,
my success.

My medium is of you entirely.
I live in you
I live by you
I live for you
Close yourself
and watch everything choke instantly.

I am all yours
Turn me into what you want
Do dare destroy me
if my defects are cumbersome
But I beg you
leave me the sap of your love
so that I can be reborn
in your ways
to your design
according to your dreams.

                        You are omnipotent.

∞∞

Solar eclipse

Today
that you're away
visiting with Yolie,
your lovely
sis, in Oregon,
the sun has risen
in the Northwest, opposite
its usual site,
far away from
our home
in Tarpon Springs, Florida.
It is dark
in my heart, where night
crashed
this morning.
I miss you much my darling.
Cannot wait
for our date.

Deserted beach, 24 x 36, oil on canvas

My sun

My love, my sun
Tambour of my fun
Star of my dark night
do not leave tonight
freeze on my horizon
I do not live when you're gone

I like when you're shining
I like when you're burning
I love when your beam
penetrates and fires me

I do not know why
the cloudy sky
why everything
is changing

My love, my light
do not set tonight
stay frozen
on my horizon
I die every time
you are sad
every time
you turn off
every time
you leave me

To
my wife, children, relatives,
friends, colleagues...

Epitaph

To all of you
who loved me
and contributed to make my life enjoyable
I would like to say before being buried:
thank you from the bottom of my heart.

It's true I was human, I was very human
and as such I was not perfect.
I made regrettable mistakes,
but I had never been content
with my imperfection.
All my life I have fought a fierce fight
against everything that was vile in me
and, without underestimating my attributes
and having took them for granted,
while having appreciated
and been grateful to have been privileged
among so many unfortunate
and disinherited people on this earth,
while rejoicing to exist
and enjoying living,
I constantly introspected
and did self-criticism.

I worked hard to develop my talents
and I tried to polish my virtues
to shine the best of myself.

If I ever offended you
by my remarks
my comments
my actions
my behavior
my ways…
to you, my loves
and to all those
who had unfortunately suffered
from my offenses
I ask for forgiveness.
It has always been far,
very far from my intention
to hurt anyone.
I never stopped loving you.

I would like to leave with the hope
that I will continue to flourish forever
in your heart
and that my grave
will remain to you a party hall
where you will celebrate my good deeds
and what was great in me.

∞∞

∞∞

www.ingramcontent.com/pod-product-compliance
Lightning Source LLC
Chambersburg PA
CBHW062028290426
44108CB00025B/2823